MW01233918

To the Extreme

Aggressive In-Line Skating

by Angie Peterson Kaelberer

Reading Consultant:
Barbara J. Fox
Reading Specialist
North Carolina State University

Capstone
press

Mankato, Minnesota

Blazers is published by Capstone Press,
151 Good Counsel Drive, P.O. Box 669, Mankato, Minnesota 56002.
www.capstonepress.com

Library of Congress Cataloging-in-Publication Data
Kaelberer, Angie Peterson.
   Aggressive in-line skating / by Angie Peterson Kaelberer.
   p. cm.—(Blazers. To the extreme)
   Summary: "Describes the sport of aggressive in-line skating,
including equipment, tricks, and safety information"—Provided
by publisher.
   Includes bibliographical references and index.
   ISBN-13: 978-0-7368-4396-6 (hardcover)
   ISBN-10: 0-7368-4396-5 (hardcover)
   ISBN-13: 978-0-7368-6173-1 (softcover)
   ISBN-10: 0-7368-6173-4 (softcover)
   1. In-line skating—Juvenile literature. I. Title. II. Series.
GV859.73.K34 2006
796.21—dc22   2005001430

Credits
Jason Knudson, set designer; Kate Opseth, book designer; Jo Miller,
   photo researcher; Scott Thoms, photo editor

Photo Credits
Corbis/Duomo/Chris Trotman, 5, 14, 15, 16–17, 19, 28–29;
   NewSport/Al Fuchs, 9; Larry Kasperek, 8
Getty Images Inc./Stanley Chou, cover, 6, 12, 20, 22, 23, 26
Patrick Batchelder, 11, 13, 25

Table of Contents

Best Trick Competition

In-line skaters and fans gather for the competition. The first skater soars high above a halfpipe ramp. He grabs one skate with his hand.

Halfpipe ramp

Another skater takes his turn
on the ramp. He combines a grab
with a flip.

BLAZER FACT

Hockey players used
the first in-line skates
to practice in summer.

Marc Englehart perfectly lands his last trick. The judges give him the highest score. Englehart wins the gold medal.

Skating Styles

Vert skaters do tricks on large halfpipe ramps. The skaters reach heights of 10 feet (3 meters) above the ramp.

Wedge ramp

Park skaters try out their moves
in skateparks and on city streets.
They do tricks on wedge ramps,
benches, and stair rails.

Skaters show off their tricks at competitions. Top skaters compete for money and prizes.

A skater does a method invert with just one hand on the ramp.

Method invert

In-Line Skater Diagram

Helmet

Halfpipe ramp

Skate boot

EXPN INVITATIONAL
expn.com ESPN ESPN
Gwinnett County, GA

Wheel

Coping

Tricks

Vert skaters use ramps to get into the air. They spin and flip. They do grinds on the edge of the ramp. This edge is called the coping.

Park skaters do grinds on obstacles like stair rails. Their skates slide along the obstacle.

BLAZER FACT

Park skating competitions have obstacles like those on city streets.

Both vert and park skaters do
grabs. They grab their skates with
one or both hands.

BLAZER FACT

Aggressive in-line skates
have a grind plate
between the second
and third wheels.

Grind plate

Grab

safety

Even the best skaters can fall.
Helmets protect their heads. Pads
cushion their elbows and knees.

In-line tricks are daring but can be dangerous. Skaters practice tricks many times to do them safely.

BLAZER FACT

Vert skaters wear both helmets and pads in most competitions. Park skaters sometimes don't wear pads.

Glossary

competition (kom-puh-TISH-uhn)—a contest between two or more people

flip (FLIP)—a trick that looks like a somersault in the air; skaters do forward and backward flips.

grab (GRAB)—a trick during which a skater grabs the skates

grind (GRINDE)—a trick performed by sliding the skate's wheels over an object, such as a railing

halfpipe ramp (HAF-pipe RAMP)—a U-shaped ramp with high walls

obstacle (OB-stuh-kuhl)—an object such as a curb or a railing; skaters perform tricks on obstacles.

vert skating (VURT SKAY-ting)—a skating style performed on halfpipe ramps

Read More

Blomquist, Christopher. *In-line Skating in the X Games.* A Kid's Guide to the X Games. New York: PowerKids Press, 2003.

Crossingham, John, and Bobbie Kalman. *Extreme In-line Skating.* Extreme Sports No Limits! New York: Crabtree, 2004.

Weil, Ann. *Aggressive In-line Skating.* X-Sports. Mankato, Minn.: Capstone Press, 2005.

Internet Sites

FactHound offers a safe, fun way to find Internet sites related to this book. All of the sites on FactHound have been researched by our staff.

Here's how:

1. Visit *www.facthound.com*
2. Type in this special code **0736843965** for age-appropriate sites. Or enter a search word related to this book for a more general search.
3. Click on the **Fetch It** button.

FactHound will fetch the best sites for you!

Index